W9-BWF-395

DATE DUE

Finding Colors

Blue

Moira Anderson

Heinemann Library
Chicago, Illinois

© 2006 Heinemann Library
a division of Reed Elsevier Inc.
Chicago, Illinois

Customer Service 888-454-2279
Visit our website at www.heinemannlibrary.com

Editorial: Moira Anderson, Carmel Heron
Page layout: Marta White, Heinemann Library Australia
Photo research: Jes Senbergs, Wendy Duncan
Production: Tracey Jarrett
Printed and bound in China by South China Printing Company Ltd.

09 08 07 06
10 9 8 7 6 5 4 3 2 1

Library of Congress Cataloging-in-Publication Data
Anderson, Moira (Moira Wilshin)
 Blue / Moira Anderson.
      p. cm. -- (Finding colors)
 Includes bibliographical references and index.
  ISBN 1-4034-7444-3 (lib. bdg. : alk. paper) -- ISBN 1-4034-7449-4 (pbk. : alk. paper)
 1. Blue--Juvenile literature. 2. Colors--Juvenile literature. I. Title.
II. Series: Anderson, Moira (Moira Wilshin). Finding colors.
 QC495.5.A533 2005
 535.6--dc22

                                                  2005009722

Acknowledgments
The author and publisher are grateful to the following for permission to reproduce copyright material: Rob Cruse Photography: pp. **5** (all items), **6, 8, 9, 10, 11** (party hat), **13, 14, 15, 23** (bottle, pencil case); Corbis: p. **17**; Getty Images/PhotoDisc: p. **18**; PhotoDisc: pp. **4, 7, 11** (balloon), **12, 16, 19, 21, 23** (globe); photolibrary.com: pp. **20, 22, 23** (beaks, feathers).

Front cover photograph permission of Tudor Photography, back cover photographs permission of PhotoDisc (starfish) and Rob Cruse Photography (teddy bear).

Every effort has been made to contact copyright holders of any material reproduced in this book. Any omissions will be rectified in subsequent printings if notice is given to the publisher.

Many thanks to the teachers, library media specialists, reading instructors, and educational consultants who have helped develop the Read and Learn/Lee y aprende brand.

Contents

Some words are shown in bold, **like this**.
You can find them in the glossary on page 23.

What Is Blue?

Blue is a color.

What different colors can you see in this picture?

The color blue is all around.

Have you seen these blue things?

What Blue Things Are There at Home?

Toys can be blue.

This teddy bear is soft and cuddly.

Bowls can be blue.

This blue bowl is used for oatmeal.

What Is Blue out My Window?

The sky looks blue out the window.

The sky is mostly blue when it is daytime and there are no clouds.

This blue car is on the road out the window.

It moves fast along the road.

What Blue Things Can I Have at My Party?

This present is blue.

It has a blue ribbon and wrapping paper.

Some party hats and balloons
are blue.

The hats are made of shiny blue
cardboard.

What Blue Things Do I Use at School?

There is a **globe** of the world at school.

The blue parts of the globe show the ocean.

This blue bottle is good for keeping
a drink.

It is made of **plastic** so it won't break.

What Else Is Blue at School?

zipper

Pencils can be kept in a blue pencil case.

The blue **zipper** can open and close the case.

Blue pencils are used at school.

They are good for drawing blue sky.

What Is Blue at the Beach?

The ocean can look blue at the beach.

The water is not very deep here.

These beach umbrellas are blue.

They protect people from the sun.

What Blue Things Do People Use?

This vase is blue.

People use vases for flowers.

People use blue ribbons for prizes.

A blue ribbon is for first prize.

Are There Blue Animals?

beaks

feathers

These birds are blue.

They clean their **feathers** with their **beaks**.

This starfish is blue.

It has a body in the middle and five arms.

Quiz

What blue things can you see at this party?

Look for the answers on page 24.

Glossary

beak
hard part of a bird's mouth

feather
light covering that grows from
a bird's skin

globe
ball shape with a map
of the world on it

plastic
strong, light material that can be
made into different shapes

zipper
used to join two pieces of material
together; used in bags and clothes

Index

Answers to the quiz on page 22

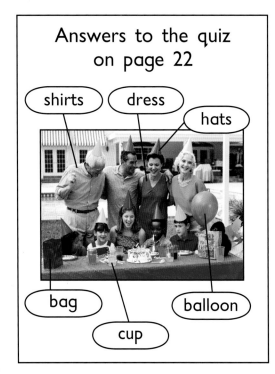

shirts

dress

hats

bag

cup

balloon

Notes to parents and teachers

Reading non-fiction texts for information is an important part of a child's literacy development. Readers can be encouraged to ask simple questions and then use the text to find the answers. Each chapter in this book begins with a question. Read the questions together. Look at the pictures. Talk about what the answer might be. Then read the text to find out if your predictions were correct. To develop readers' enquiry skills, encourage them to think of other questions they might ask about the topic. Discuss where you could find the answers. Assist children in using the contents page, picture glossary and index to practise research skills and new vocabulary.